Welcome to the Forest

by Ruth Owen

Peachtree

Published in 2016 by Ruby Tuesday Books Ltd.

Editor: Mark J. Sachner
Designer: Emma Randall
Consultant: Judy Wearing, PhD, BEd
Production: John Lingham

Photo credits
Alamy: 15 (center), 16, 24 (right), 25, 27 (top), 30; Corbis: 18 (top); FLPA: 9 (right), 11 (left), 12 (right), 13 (bottom), 17, 29, 30; Public Domain: 15 (top), 15 (bottom); Shutterstock: Cover, 2–3, 4–5, 6–7, 8, 9 (left), 10, 11 (right), 12 (left), 13 (top), 14 (bottom), 14–15 (center), 18 (bottom), 19, 20–21, 22–23, 24 (top), 24 (left), 25 (bottom left), 26, 27 (bottom), 28, 30, 31.

Library of Congress Control Number: 2015916858

ISBN 978-1-910549-64-3

Printed and published in the United States of America

For further information including rights and permissions requests, please contact our Customer Service Department at 877-337-8577.

Contents

Words shown in **bold** in the text are explained in the glossary.

Welcome to the Forest

Who and what lives in a forest?

This **habitat** is home to trees, moss, and **fungi**.

The residents of this habitat include raccoons, birds, spiders, and other animals.

Every living thing in the forest gets what it needs to live from its habitat.

A forest is a type of ecosystem. An ecosystem includes all the living things in an area. It also includes non-living things such as soil, rocks, sunlight, and rain. Everything in an ecosystem has its own part to play.

So let's find out what happens in this natural neighborhood ...
... welcome to the forest!

Acorns, Shoots, Leaves, and Roots

It's spring in the forest, and fat buds are growing on the branches of trees.

When the buds burst open, leaves uncurl from inside.

If you visit a forest, you might not notice the soil. Without it, however, the trees and other plants could not live. Plants take in water and **nutrients** from soil through their roots.

Bud

Oak tree leaves

These tree roots grow deep into the soil.

Rainwater soaks into the soil.

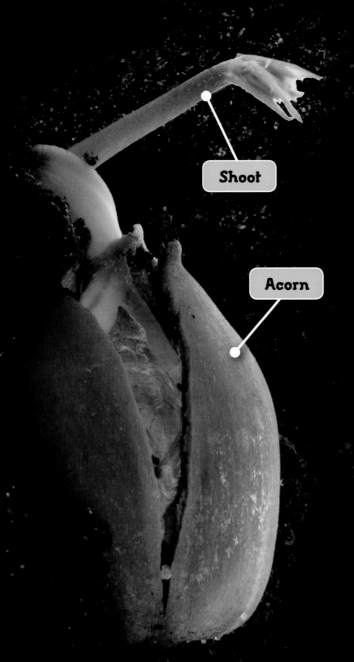

Shoot

Acorn

An acorn is buried in the forest soil.

Once the spring sunshine warms the soil, a **shoot** starts to grow.

Seedling

Within a few weeks, the shoot grows into an oak tree seedling.

Once the oak tree is fully grown, it may live for hundreds of years!

In what ways do you think the forest trees are helpful to animals?

Tree Trunk Nests

Peck. Peck. Peck. A woodpecker is pecking a nest hole in a tree trunk.

Woodpecker

Making the hole will take him up to six weeks!

Once the nest is ready, his partner lays her eggs inside.

Nest hole

Parent woodpeckers take turns sitting on their eggs. The eggs must be kept warm so the chicks inside can grow.

In another tree trunk, a squirrel has found a cozy hole and made it her nest.

Mother squirrel feeding kits

Inside the nest, she gives birth to four tiny babies, called kits.

She feeds the kits with milk from her body.

Where else do animals live in the forest?

Life on the Forest Floor

Not every forest animal lives in the trees—many live on the forest floor.

Deer move quietly among the trees, feeding on leaves, berries, nuts, grasses, and flowers.

Deer

A timber rattlesnake waits for mice and other small animals to pass by.

Its colors and pattern are good **camouflage** that help it blend in with the forest floor.

When its **prey** comes near, the snake attacks with a deadly bite.

Blue spotted salamander

Timber rattlesnake

Blue spotted salamanders spend their time in damp places, such as under rocks and on rotting logs. They hunt for insects, spiders, worms, and slugs.

What animals do you think hunt for food in the forest as night falls?

The Forest at Night

It's evening in the forest, and a pair of raccoon cubs are playing in the trees.

Raccoon cub

Mother raccoon

Their mother looks for bird nests in tree holes, so the family can feed on eggs.

When night falls, raccoons go looking for food. They eat leaves, berries, seeds, insects, and eggs. They even feed on the dead bodies of other animals.

A barred owl feeding on a crow

A barred owl sits on a branch watching for prey such as mice, squirrels, and birds.

He swoops through the trees and grabs his prey with his sharp claws, called talons.

Bat

Moth

When night falls, bats fly through the darkness hunting for moths and other insects.

Where do ants build nests in a forest?

13

Forest Minibeasts

A forest is home to millions of insects and spiders.

Carpenter ants make their nests in rotting logs and dead tree stumps.

Using their mouthparts, they chew tunnels and nesting areas in wood.

Carpenter ant

Mouthparts

A horntail lays her eggs in a tree trunk. She pushes her long, tube-like **ovipositor** into the tree. Then her eggs pass down the tube into the wood. When **larvae** hatch from the eggs, they feed on wood.

Horntail

Ovipositor

Larva

Wolf spider

Grasshopper

Wolf spiders hunt insects by hiding on the forest floor and then pouncing on their prey.

What bird hunts for ants to feed to its chicks?

Hungry Forest Babies

Nest

In the tree hole nest, the woodpecker chicks have hatched from their eggs.

Chick

Mother woodpecker

Father woodpecker catching ants

The parent woodpeckers catch carpenter ants, larvae, and other insects to feed to the chicks.

The adult woodpeckers eat insects, berries, and nuts.

The squirrel kits are now seven weeks old.

When their mother leaves the nest to find food, the kits go, too.

Squirrels eat leaves, shoots, roots, flowers, seeds, and nuts. They also feed on tree bark and fungi.

A squirrel kit eating fungi

Fungi

When a forest animal dies, what do you think happens to its body?

17

Becoming Part of the Forest

A deer has died in the forest.

Now, the deer's body will become food for other forest animals.

The raccoon family visits the body and eats some meat.

Flies and beetles lay their eggs on the body.

18

When fly and beetle larvae hatch from
the eggs, they feed on the body, too.

Fly larvae

In time, the body breaks down and
rots until all that's left are bones.

Tiny bits of
a rotting body get
mixed into the soil.
They add nutrients to
the soil that plants need
to grow and be healthy.
Plants take in the
nutrients with
their roots.

Fungi help with recycling in a forest.
What do you think they recycle?

19

Forest Fungi

Dead, rotting tree trunk

When a tree dies, fungi, such as mushrooms, grow on the tree.

The fungi get nutrients from the dead tree.

Fungi

As fungi spread and feed on a dead tree, they make the wood rot and become crumbly.

In time, the rotting wood becomes part of the forest soil.

When the wood is recycled into soil, it adds nutrients that living trees and other plants need.

Some types of fungi grow on dead wood. Others grow on live trees, and some grow in soil. Many fungi are poisonous. So never touch fungi you see growing in a forest, field, or any other outdoor place.

Fungi

What tiny forest plant grows on tree trunks, branches, rotting logs, and rocks?

A Carpet of Moss

In a cool, damp forest, moss grows on many trees, logs, and rocks.

A carpet-like covering of moss is made up of thousands of tiny plants.

Moss

Each individual moss plant has a single stem and tiny leaves.

Moss is useful to many forest creatures.

Insects and spiders take shelter in moss.

Mice, birds, and other animals collect soft moss to put in their nests.

Water bear

Mouse

Water bears, or moss piglets, are **microscopic** animals that live in moss. A clump of moss the size of a muffin can be home to 100,000 of these creatures!

What do the forest trees produce in summer?

23

A Time for Seeds

It's late summer, and the forest trees have grown seeds.

Oak tree seeds, which are called acorns, drop to the forest floor.

Cones filled with seeds fall from **evergreen** trees.

Acorns

Seeds

Cone

Some of the seeds will one day grow into new trees.

Others become food for mice, squirrels, raccoons, deer, and birds.

A squirrel burying an acorn

Squirrels bury acorns and other seeds in the ground. In winter, when it's hard to find seeds, they dig up this stored food. Squirrels don't find all the seeds, though, so many grow into new trees.

Acorn

What else drops from trees in the fall?

Autumn in the Forest

When fall arrives, the leaves on many trees turn yellow, orange, red, and brown.

Soon, the leaves start to fall from the trees.

This photo of a forest was taken by a person in a plane.

Millipedes on the forest floor munch on dead leaves.

Their leafy poop, which is filled with nutrients, gets mixed into the soil.

In time, the autumn leaves will rot and become new soil.

Millipede

Some of the forest trees are evergreens. These trees don't lose all their needle-like leaves in the fall. Instead, they lose and regrow some of their leaves all year round.

Evergreen tree needles

What do you think deer eat in the winter forest?

Winter Comes Around

It's winter, and a blanket of snow covers the forest.

There's not much to eat, so deer nibble on twigs and tree bark.

During winter, many of the forest trees look as if they have died. They are just resting, though. In spring, they will grow new shoots and leaves.

A raccoon finds
a cozy tree hole.

Here it will rest
and sleep for
weeks at a time.

For now the
forest is still
and white.

But soon it will be spring again ....

A Forest Food Web

A food web shows who eats who in an ecosystem.

This food web diagram shows the connections between some of the living things in a forest.

Plants make the food they need for energy and growth in their leaves. To do this they need sunlight.

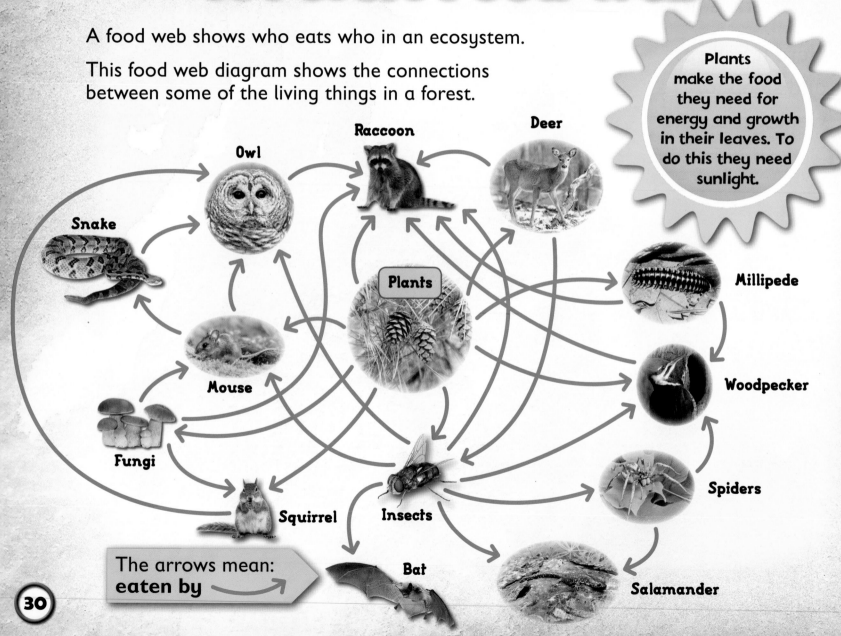

Owl

Snake

Raccoon

Deer

Millipede

Plants

Mouse

Woodpecker

Fungi

Spiders

Squirrel

Insects

Bat

Salamander

The arrows mean: **eaten by** →

Glossary

camouflage (KAM-uh-flahzh) The colors and markings of an animal that help it blend in with its habitat.

evergreen (EV-ur-green) Having green leaves all year round.

fungi (FUHN-jye) A group of living things that includes mushrooms, toadstools, and molds.

habitat (HAB-uh-tat) The place where an animal or plant lives. A habitat can be a forest, a backyard, a desert, or the ocean.

larva (LAR-vuh) A young insect that looks like a worm.

microscopic (mye-kruh-SKOP-ik) Able to be seen only with a microscope, not with the eyes alone.

nutrient (NOO-tree-uhnt) A substance that a living thing needs to grow, get energy, and be healthy.

ovipositor (oh-vih-PAH-zih-tur) A tube-like body part used by a female insect for laying eggs.

prey (PRAY) An animal that is hunted by other animals for food.

shoot (SHOOT) A new part that grows on a plant or from a seed. Shoots can become new stems or leaves.

Index

A
acorns 6–7, 24–25
ants 13, 14–15, 16

B
bats 13, 30
birds 4, 8, 12–13, 15, 16, 23, 25, 30

D
dead animals 12, 17, 18–19
deer 10, 18–19, 25, 27, 28, 30

E
ecosystems 5, 30
eggs 8, 12, 15, 16, 18–19

F
fungi 4, 17, 19, 20–21, 30

H
horntails 15

I
insects 11, 12–13, 14–15, 16, 18–19, 23, 30

M
mice 11, 13, 23, 25, 30

millipedes 27, 30
moss 4, 22–23

N
nests 8–9, 12–13, 14, 16–17, 23

R
raccoons 4–5, 12, 18, 25, 29, 30

S
salamanders 11, 30
seeds 6–7, 12, 17, 24–25
snakes 11, 30

soil 5, 6–7, 19, 21, 27
spiders 4, 11, 14–15, 23, 30
squirrels 9, 13, 17, 25, 30

T
trees 4–5, 6–7, 8–9, 10, 12–13, 14–15, 16, 20–21, 22–23, 24–25, 26–27, 28–29

W
water bears 23
woodpeckers 8, 16, 30

Read More

Phillips, Dee. *Woodpecker (Treed: Animal Life in the Trees)*. New York: Bearport Publishing (2014).

Underwood, Deborah. *Hiding in Forests (Creature Camouflage)*. Mankato, MN: Heinemann-Raintree (2011).

Learn More Online

To learn more about life in a forest, go to
www.rubytuesdaybooks.com/habitats